The International Library of Philosophy

MISUSE OF MIND

Founded by C. K. Ogden

The International Library of Philosophy

EPISTEMOLOGY AND METAPHYSICS
In 5 Volumes

I	The History of Materialism	*Lange*
II	The Structure of Metaphysics	*Lazerowitz*
III	Conditions of Knowing	*Sinclair*
IV	Misuse of Mind	*Stephen*
V	The Philosophy of "As if"	*Vaihinger*

MISUSE OF MIND

A Study of Bergson's Attack on Intellectualism

KARIN STEPHEN

With a Prefatory Letter by Henri Bergson

ROUTLEDGE
Taylor & Francis Group

First published in 1922 by
Kegan Paul, Trench, Trubner & Co Ltd

Reprinted 2000, 2001 (twice) by
Routledge

2 Park Square, Milton Park, Abingdon, Oxfordshire, OX14 4RN
270 Madison Avenue, New York NY 10016

Routledge is an imprint of the Taylor & Francis Group

First issued in paperback 2010

British Library Cataloguing in Publication Data
A CIP catalogue record for this book
is available from the British Library

Misuse of Mind

ISBN 13: 978-0-415-22528-1 (hbk)
ISBN 13: 978-0-415-61381-1 (pbk)

Epistemology and Metaphysics: 5 Volumes
ISBN 13: 978-0-415-22572-4
The International Library of Philosophy: 56 Volumes
ISBN 13: 978-0-415-21803-0

PREFATORY NOTE

Being an extract from a letter by Professor Henri Bergson

AYANT lu de près le travail de Mrs. Stephen je le trouve intéressant au plus haut point. C'est une interprétation personelle et originale de l'ensemble de mes vues—interprétation qui vaut par elle-même, indépendamment de ce qui j' ai écrit. L'auteur s'est assimilé *l'esprit* de la doctrine, puis, se dégageant de la matérialité du texte elle a développé à sa manière, dans la direction qu'elle avait choisi, des idées qui lui paraissaient fundamentales. Grace à la distinction qu'elle établit entre " fact " et " matter," elle a pu ramener à l'unité, et présenter avec une grande rigueur logique, des vues que j'avais été obligé, en raison de ma méthode de recherche, d'isoler les unes des autres. Bref, son travail a une grande valeur ; il témoigne d'une rare force de pensée.

HENRI BERGSON.

To Professor Henri Bergson
With respect and gratitude

CONTENTS

PREFACE

THE immense popularity which Bergson's philosophy enjoys is sometimes cast up against him, by those who do not agree with him, as a reproach. It has been suggested that Bergson's writings are welcomed simply because they offer a theoretical justification for a tendency which is natural in all of us but against which philosophy has always fought, the tendency to throw reason overboard and just let ourselves go. Bergson is regarded by rationalists almost as a traitor to philosophy, or as a Bolshevik inciting the public to overthrow what it has taken years of painful effort to build up.

It is possible that some people who do not understand this philosophy may use Bergson's name as a cloak for giving up all self-direction and letting themselves go intellectually to pieces, just as hooligans may use a time of revolution to plunder in the name of the Red Guard. But Bergson's philosophy is in reality as far from teaching mere laziness as Communism is from being mere destruction of the old social order.

Bergson attacks the use to which we usually put our minds, but he most certainly does not suggest that a philosopher should not use his mind at all; he is to use it for all it is worth, only differently, more efficiently for the purpose he has in view, the purpose of knowing for its own sake.

There is, of course, a sense in which doing anything in the right way is simply letting one's self go, for after all it is easier to do a thing well than badly—it certainly takes much less effort to produce the same amount of result. So to know in the way which Bergson recommends does in a sense come more easily than attempting to get the knowledge we want by inappropriate methods. If this saving of waste effort is a fault, then Bergson must plead guilty. But as the field of knowledge open to us is far too wide for any one mind to explore, the new method of knowing, though it requires less effort than the old to produce the same result, does not thereby let us off more easily, for with a better instrument it becomes possible to work for a greater result.

It is not because it affords an excuse for laziness that Bergson's philosophy is popular but because it gives expression to a feeling which is very widespread at the present time, a distrust of systems, theories, logical constructions, the assumption of premisses and then the acceptance of everything that follows logically from them. There is a sense of impatience with thought and a thirst for the actual, the concrete. It is because the whole drift of Bergson's writing is an incitement to throw over abstractions and get back to facts that so many people read him, hoping that he will put into words and find an answer to the unformulated doubt that haunts them.

It was in this spirit that the writer undertook the study of Bergson. On the first reading he appeared at once too persuasive and too vague, specious and unsatisfying: a closer investigation revealed more and more a coherent theory of reality and a new and promising method of investigating it. The apparent unsatisfactoriness of the first reading arose from a failure to realize how entirely new and unfamiliar the point of view is from which Bergson approaches metaphysical speculation. In order to understand Bergson it is necessary to adopt his attitude and that is just the difficulty, for his attitude is the exact reverse of that which has been inculcated in us by the traditions of our language and education and now comes to us naturally. This common sense attitude is based on certain assumptions which are so familiar that we simply take them for granted without expressly formulating them, and indeed, for the most part, without even realizing that we have been making any assumptions at all.

Bergson's principal aim is to direct our attention to the reality which he believes we all actually know already, but misinterpret and disregard because we are biassed by preconceived ideas. To do this Bergson has to offer some description of what this reality is, and this description will be intelligible only if we are willing and able to make a profound change in our attitude, to lay aside the old assumptions which underlie our every day common sense point of view and adopt, at least for the time being, the assumptions from which Bergson sets out. This book begins with an attempt to give as precise an account as possible of the old assumptions which we must discard and the new ones which we must adopt in order to understand Bergson's description of reality. To make the complete reversal of our ordinary mental habits needed for understanding what Bergson has to say requires a very considerable effort from anyone, but the feat is perhaps most difficult of all for those who have carefully trained themselves in habits of rigorous logical criticism. In attempting to describe what we actually know in the abstract logical terms which are the only means of intercommunication that human beings possess, Bergson is driven into perpetual self-contradiction, indeed, paradoxical though it may sound, unless he contradicted himself his description could not be a true one. It is easier for the ordinary reader to pass over the self contradictions, hardly even being aware of them, and grasp the underlying meaning: the trained logician is at once pulled up by the nonsensical form of the description and the meaning is lost in a welter of conflicting words. This, I think, is the real reason why some of the most brilliant intellectual thinkers have been able to make nothing of Bergson s philosophy: baffled by the self-contradictions into which he is necessarily driven in the attempt to convey his meaning they have hastily assumed that Bergson had no meaning to convey.

The object of this book is to set out the relation between explanations and the actual facts which we want to explain and thereby to show exactly why Bergson *must* use self-contradictory terms if the explanation of reality which he offers is to be a true one.

Having first shown what attitude Bergson requires us to adopt I have gone on to describe what he thinks this new way of looking at reality will reveal. This at once involves me in the difficulty with which Bergson wrestles in all his attempts to describe reality, the difficulty which arises from the fundamental discrepancy between what he sees the actual fact to be and the abstract notions which are all he has with which to describe it. I have attempted to show how it comes about that we are in fact able to perform this apparently impossible feat of describing the indescribable, using Bergson's descriptions of sensible perception and the relations of matter and memory to illustrate my point. If we succeed in ridding ourselves of our common-sense preconceptions, Bergson tells us that we may expect to know the old facts in a new way, face to face, as it were, instead of seeing them through a web of our own intellectual interpretations. I have not attempted to offer any proof whether or not Bergson's description of reality is in fact true: having understood the meaning of the description it remains for each of us to decide for himself whether or not it fits the facts.

KARIN STEPHEN.

Cambridge, January, 1922.

CHAPTER I

EXPLANATION

In order to understand Bergson it is not necessary to have any previous acquaintance with philosophy, indeed the less the reader knows of current metaphysical notions the easier it may perhaps be for him to adopt the mental attitude required for understanding Bergson. For Bergson says that the tradition of philosophy is all wrong and must be broken with: according to his view philosophical knowledge can only be obtained by "a reversal of the usual work of the intellect."*

The usual work of the intellect consists in analysis and classification: if you have anything presented to you which you do not understand the obvious question to put yourself is, "what is it?" Suppose in a dark room which you expected to find empty you stumble against something, the natural thing to do is to begin at once to try to fit your experience into some class already familiar to you. You find it has a certain texture which you class as rather rough, a temperature

* *Introduction to Metaphysics*, page 34.

which you class as warm, a size which you class as about two feet high, a peculiar smell which you recognise and you finally jump to the answer to your question : it is " a dog." This intellectual operation is a sample of the way in which it comes natural to us to set to work whenever we find ourselves confronted with any situation which we are not able to classify off hand, we are not easy till we can say *what* the situation is, and saying *what* consists in hitting upon some class with which we are already familiar to which it belongs : in this instance the question was answered when you succeeded in describing the situation to yourself as "stumbling upon a dog." Now you were only able to class what was stumbled upon as a dog after you had recognised a certain number of properties as being those shared by dogs—the rough texture, the size, the smell. You analysed the situation as containing these qualities and thereupon classified what had been stumbled upon as a dog.

Analysis and classification are the two methods which we are accustomed to rely upon for improving our knowledge in unfamiliar situations and we are accustomed to take it that they improve our knowledge of the whole situation : anyone who said that after you were able to say what you had stumbled upon you knew less of the whole situation than you knew before would find it difficult to get you to agree. And yet this is very much the position which Bergson takes up. Analysis and classification, he would admit, are the way to get more knowledge, of a kind; they enable us to describe situations and they are the starting point of all explanation and prediction. After analysis and classification you were able to say, "I have stumbled upon a dog," and having got so far you could then pass on to whatever general laws you knew of as applying to the classes into which you had fitted the situation, and by means of these laws still more of the situation could be classified and explained. Thus by means of the general law, "dogs lick," you would be furnished with an explanation if perhaps you felt something warm and damp on your hand, or again knowledge of this law might lead you to expect such a feeling. When what we want is to describe or to explain a situation in general terms then Bergson agrees that analysis and classification are the methods to employ, but he maintains that these methods which are useful for describing and explaining are no use for finding out the actual situation which we may want to describe or explain. And he goes a step further. Not only do these methods fail to reveal the situation but the intellectual attitude of abstraction to which they accustom us seriously handicaps us when we want not merely to explain the situation but to know it. Now it is the business of science to explain situations in terms of general laws and so the intellectual method of abstraction is the right one for scientists to employ. Bergson claims, however, that philosophy has a task quite distinct from that of science. In whatever situation he finds himself a man may take up one of two attitudes, he may either adopt a practical attitude, in which case he will set to work to explain the situation in order that he may know what to do under the circumstances, or he may take a speculative interest in it and then he will devote himself to knowing it simply for the sake of knowing. It is only, according to Bergson, in the former case, when his interest is practical, that he will attain his object by using the intellectual method of abstraction which proceeds by analysis and classification. These intellectual operations have such prestige, however, they have proved so successful in discovering explanations, that we are apt to take it for granted that they must be the best way to set to work whatever sort of knowledge we want : we might almost be tempted, off hand, to imagine that they were our only way of knowing at all, but a moment's reflection will show that this, at any rate, would be going too far.

Before we can analyse and classify and explain we must have something to analyse, some material to work upon : these operations are based upon something which we know directly, what we see, for instance, or touch or feel. This something is the foundation of knowledge, the intellectual operations of analysis classification and the framing of general laws are simply an attempt to describe and explain it. It is the business of science to explain and intellectual methods are the appropriate ones for science to employ. But the business of philosophy, according to Bergson, is not to explain reality but to know it. For this a different kind of mental effort is required. Analysis and classification, instead of increasing our direct knowledge, tend rather to diminish it. They must always start from some direct knowledge, but they proceed, not by widening the field of this knowledge but by leaving out more and more of it. Moreover, unless we are constantly on the alert, the intellectual habit of using all our direct knowledge as material for analysis and classification ends by completely misleading us as to what it is that we do actually know. So that the better we explain the less, in the end, we know.

There can be no doubt that something is directly known but disputes break out as soon as we try to say what that something is. Is it the "real" world of material objects, or a mental copy of these objects, or are we altogether on the wrong track in looking for two kinds of realities, the "real" world and "our mental states," and is it perceived events alone that are "real?" This something which we know directly has been given various names: "the external object," "sense data," "phenomena," and so on, each more or less coloured by implications belonging to one or other of the rival theories as to what it is. We shall call it "the facts" to emphasise its indubitable reality, and avoid, as far as possible, any other implications.

Controversy about "the facts" has been mainly as to what position they occupy in the total scheme of reality. As to what they are at the moment when we are actually being acquainted with them one would have thought there could have been no two opinions; it seems impossible that we should make any mistake about that. No doubt it is impossible to have such a thing as a false experience, an experience is what it is, only judgments can be false. But it is quite possible to make a false judgment as to what experience we are actually having, or, still more commonly, simply to take for granted that our experience must be such and such, without ever looking to see whether it is or not. A small child taken to a party and told that parties are great fun if questioned afterwards will very likely say it has enjoyed itself though, if you happened to have been there, you may have seen clearly that it was really bewildered or bored. Even when we grow up names still have a tendency to impose upon us and disguise from us the actual nature of our experiences. There are not very many people who, if invited to partake, for instance, of the last bottle of some famous vintage wine, would have the courage to admit, even to themselves, that it was nasty, even though it was, in fact, considerably past its prime. Cases of this kind, with which we are all familiar, are enough to make us realize that it is actually quite possible to make mistakes even about facts which we know directly, to overlook the actual fact altogether because we have made up our minds in advance as to what it is sure to be.

Now Bergson says that such errors are not confined to stray instances, such as we have noticed, in which the imposition of preconceived ideas can readily be detected by a little closer attention to the actual facts. He believes that a falsification due to preconceived ideas, runs right through the whole of our direct experience. He lays the blame both for this falsification and for our failure to detect it upon our intellectual habit of relying upon explanation rather than upon direct knowledge, and that is one of the reasons why he says that our intellectual attitude is an obstacle to direct knowledge of the facts. The intellectual method of abstraction by which we analyse and classify is the foundation of all description and explanation in terms of general laws, and the truth is that we are, as a rule, much more preoccupied with explaining the facts which we know than with the actual experiencing of them.

This preoccupation is natural enough. The bare fact which we know directly is not enough to enable us to carry on our everyday lives, we cannot get on unless we supplement it with some sort of explanation and, if it comes to choosing between fact and explanation, the explanation is often of more practical use than the fact. So it comes about that we are inclined to use the facts which we know directly simply as material for constructing explanations and to pay so little attention to them for their own sakes that we simply take it for granted that they must be what our explanations lead us to suppose they are.

Now according to Bergson the attitude of mind required for explaining the facts conflicts with that which is required for knowing them. From the point of view simply of knowing, the facts are all equally important and we cannot afford to discriminate, but for explanation some facts are very much more important than others. When we want to explain, therefore, rather than simply to know, we tend to concentrate our attention upon these practically important facts and pass over the rest. For in order to describe and explain a situation we have to classify it, and in order to do this we must pick out in it properties required for membership of some one or other of the classes known to us. In the situation which we originally considered by way of illustration, for instance, you had to pick out the qualities of roughness, warmth and so on, in order to classify what you had stumbled upon as " a dog." Now the picking out of these particular qualities is really an operation of abstraction from the situation as a whole : they were the important features of the situation from the point of view of classifying what you had stumbled upon, but they by no means exhausted the whole situation. Our preoccupation with explaining the facts, then, leads us to treat what we know directly as so much material for abstraction.

This intellectual attitude, as Bergson calls it, though practically useful, has, according to him, two grave drawbacks from the point of view of speculation. By focussing our attention upon anything less than the whole fact, and so isolating a part from the rest, he says we distort what we knew originally : furthermore just in so far as we make a selection among the facts, attending to some and passing over others, we limit the field of direct knowledge which we might otherwise have enjoyed. For these two reasons Bergson insists that it is the business of philosophy to reverse the intellectual habit of mind and return to the fullest possible direct knowledge of the fact. " May not the task of philosophy," he says, " be to bring us back to a fuller perception of reality by a certain displacement of our attention ? What would be required would be to turn our attention *away* from the practically interesting aspect of the universe in order to turn it *back* to what, from a practical point of view, is useless. And this conversion of attention would be philosophy itself."*

At first sight it appears paradoxical and absurd to maintain that our efforts to analyse, classify and explain the facts tend rather to limit than to extend our knowledge, and furthermore distort even such facts as we still remain acquainted with. Common sense has no doubt that, far from limiting and distorting our knowledge, explanation is the only possible way in which we can get beyond the little scraps of fact which are all that we can ever know directly.

If the views of common sense on this question were formulated, which, for the most part, they are not, they would be something like this. Until we begin to think the facts which we know directly are all muddled together and confused : first of all it is necessary to sort them by picking out qualities from the general confusion in which they are at first concealed. It is possible that during this process, which is what is called analysis, we may be obliged, at first, to overlook some of what we already know in a vague sort of way, but this insignificant loss is compensated by

* *La Perception du Changement*, page 13.

the clarity of what remains, and is, in any case, only temporary. For as the analysis proceeds we gradually replace the whole of the original mere muddle by clear and definite things and qualities. At first we may be able to distinguish only a few qualities here and there, and our preoccupation with these may possibly lead us, for a time, to pay insufficient attention to the rest of the muddle which we know directly but have not yet succeeded in analysing. But when the analysis is completed the distinct things and qualities which we shall then know will contain *all* that we originally knew, and more besides, since the analysis will have revealed much that was originally concealed or only implicit in the original unanalysed fact. If, for instance, you look at a very modern painting, at first what you are directly aware of may be little more than a confused sight: bye and bye, as you go on looking, you will be able to distinguish colours and shapes, one by one objects may be recognised until finally you may be able to see the whole picture at a glance as composed of four or five different colours arranged in definite shapes and positions. You may even be able to make out that it represents a human figure, or a landscape. Common sense would tell you that if your analysis is complete these colours and shapes will exhaust the whole of what you originally knew and moreover that in the course of it much will have been discovered which originally you could hardly be said to have known at all, so that analysis, far from limiting your direct knowledge, will have added to it considerably. Starting, then, originally, from a very meagre stock of direct knowledge, analysis, according to the common sense view, by discovering more and more qualities, builds up for us more and more direct knowledge.

Bergson begins just the other way up. He starts from the idea of a whole field of direct knowledge vastly more extended than the actual facts of which we are normally aware as making up our direct experience. He calls this whole field of knowledge "virtual knowledge." This field of virtual knowledge contains the whole of the actions and reactions of matter in which our body has its part at any moment, the multitude of stimulations which actually assail the senses but which we normally disregard, together with all the responses by which our bodies adjust themselves to these stimulations, and, in addition, the whole of our past. For Bergson the problem is to explain, not how we increase our direct knowledge, but how we limit it: not how we remember, but how we forget. "Our knowledge," he says, "far from being built up by a gradual combination of simple elements, is the result of a sharp dissociation. From the infinitely vast field of our virtual knowledge we have selected, to turn into actual knowledge, whatever concerns our action upon things; the rest we have neglected. The brain appears to have been constructed on purpose for this work of selection. It is easy enough to show that this is so in the case of memory. Our past, as we shall show in the next lecture, is necessarily preserved, automatically. It survives in its entirety. But it is to our practical interest to put it aside, or at any rate only to accept just so much of it as can more or less usefully throw light on the present situation and complete it. The brain enables us to make this selection: it materialises the useful memories and keeps those which would be of no use below the threshold of consciousness. The same thing may be said of perception: perception is the servant of action and out of the whole of reality it isolates only what interests us; it shows us not so much the things themselves as what we can make of them. In advance it classifies them, in advance it arranges them; we barely look at the object, it is enough for us to know to what category it belongs."*

According to Bergson the facts which we actually know directly in the ordinary course are discriminated out of a very much wider field which we must also be said in a sense to know directly though most of it lies outside the clear focus of attention. This whole field of virtual knowledge is regarded as standing

* *La Perception du Changement*, pages 12 and 13.

to the actual facts to which we usually devote our attention, much as, for instance, the whole situation of stumbling upon something in a dark room stood to the single quality of roughness: in both cases there is a central point in the full focus of attention which we are apt to look upon as the fact directly known, but this central point is really surrounded by a vastly wider context and this too is known in some sense though it is commonly ignored.

For all philosophies, whether they be Bergson's or the view of common sense or any other, the actual facts which require to be explained are the same, and, though any positive assertion as to what these facts are may be hotly disputed, it will probably be admitted that as we ordinarily know them they consist in some direct experience, undeniable as far as it goes. The point at issue between Bergson and common sense is, precisely, how far it does go. Both sides would admit that, in this fact directly known, what is in the full focus of attention at any given moment is very limited; on the other hand both would admit that this fully focussed fact is set in a context, or fringe, with no clearly defined limits which also goes to make up the whole fact directly known though we do not usually pay much attention to it. The fact directly known being given the problem is to find out what it is and how it comes to be known. What is actually given and needs to be accounted for is the fact clearly focussed, with its less clearly defined fringe: Bergson's sweeping assumption of the existence of a further vast field of virtual knowledge in order to account for it, does, at first sight, seem arbitrary and unwarranted and in need of considerable justification before it can be accepted. For him the problem then becomes, not to account for our knowing as much as we do, but to see why it is that we do not know a great deal more: why our actual knowledge does not cover the whole field of our virtual knowledge. Common sense, on the other hand, sets out from the assumption of ignorance, absence of awareness, as being, as it were, natural and not needing any accounting for, and so it regards the problem as being to explain why any experience ever occurs at all. The assumption of ignorance as being the natural thing seems at first sight to need no justification, but this may well be due merely to our having grown accustomed to the common sense point of view. When one begins to question this assumption it begins to appear just as arbitrary as the contrary standpoint adopted by Bergson. The actual facts are neither ignorance nor full knowledge and in accounting for them it is really just as arbitrary to assume one of these two extremes as the other. The truth appears to be that in order to account for the facts one must make some assumptions, and these, not being facts actually given, are bound to be more or less arbitrary. They seem more or less "natural" according as we are more or less accustomed to the idea of them, but they are really justified only according to the success with which they account for the actual facts.

This idea of putting the problem of knowledge in terms exactly the reverse of those in which it seems "natural" to put it was originally suggested to Bergson by his study of the important work on amnesia carried out by Charcot and his pupils, and also by such evidence as was to be had at the time when he wrote on the curious memory phenomena revealed by the use of hypnotism and by cases of spontaneous dissociation. It is impossible to prove experimentally that no experience is ever destroyed but it is becoming more and more firmly established that enormous numbers of past experiences, which are inaccessible to ordinary memory and which therefore it would seem "natural" to suppose destroyed, can, if the right methods are employed, be revived even with amazing fullness of detail.

In recent years since Bergson's books were first published, great strides have been made in the experimental investigation of the whole subject of memory, and the evidence thus obtained, far from upsetting the theory of memory suggested to him by the less extensive evidence which was available at the time when he wrote, lends it striking support.

It appears to be accepted by doctors who use hypnotism in psychotherapy that under hypnotism many patients can perfectly well be taken back in memory to any period of their lives which the doctor chooses to ask for, and can be made not only to remember vaguely a few incidents which occurred at the time but actually to re-live the whole period in the fullest possible detail, feeling over again with hallucinatory vividness all the emotions experienced at the time.

This re-living of past experience can, with some patients, be made to go on indefinitely, through the whole day, if the doctor has time to attend to it, every little incident being faithfully recalled though the actual event may have taken place 20 or 30 years previously. And this happens not simply in the case of some very striking event or great crisis which the patient has been through, indeed it is just the striking events that are often hardest to recover. Some doctors, in order to get at the crisis, have found it useful occasionally to put patients back through one birthday after another right back even as early as their second year, to see at what point in their lives some particular nervous symptom first appeared, and each successive birthday is lived through again in the utmost detail.*

Evidence of this kind does not, of course, prove that literally *nothing* is ever lost but it

*See *Psychology and Psychotherapy* by Dr. William Brown.

goes far towards upsetting the ordinary view that it is the rule for past experience to be annihilated and the exception for fragments here and there to be preserved in memory. The evidence which has so far been collected and which is rapidly accumulating at least seems to justify us in reversing this rule and saying rather that to be preserved is the rule for experience and to be lost would be the exception, if indeed any experience ever really is lost at all.

This way of regarding the field of memory is further supported by such evidence as has been collected with regard to the influence of past experience in dreams, phobias and various forms of insanity, but in these cases, of course, it is only isolated past experiences here and there whose activity can be observed, and so, while helping to upset the most natural assumption that whatever cannot be recalled by ordinary efforts of memory may be assumed to have been destroyed, they do not lend very much support to the wider view put forward by Bergson, that no experience, however trivial, is ever destroyed but that all of it is included in the field out of which memory makes its practical selection.

Taking all the evidence with regard to the preservation of past experience which is at present available, then, it is safe to say that, while it cannot, in the nature of things, absolutely prove Bergson's theory of knowledge, it in no way conflicts with it and even supports it, positively in the sense that the theory does fit the facts well enough to explain them (though it goes further than the actual facts and makes assumptions which can neither be proved nor disproved by an appeal to them) and negatively in the sense that what we now know about memory actually conflicts with the "natural" view that past experience which we are unable to recall has been destroyed, which is commonly appealed to to show the absurdity of the rival theory put forward by Bergson.

On the assumption which Bergson makes of a much wider field of direct knowledge than that which contains what we are accustomed to regard as the actual facts which we know directly, Bergson's problem becomes how to account for these facts being so much less than the whole field which we might have expected to have known. The answer, according to him, is to be found in our practical need of being prepared in advance for what is to come, at whatever sacrifice of direct knowledge of past and present facts. For practical purposes it is essential to use present and past facts as signs of what is coming so that we may be ready for it. To this end it is far more important to know the general laws according to which facts occur than to experience the facts themselves in their fullness. Our intellectual habits which prompt us to set to work at once in every unfamiliar situation to analyse and classify it fit us for discovering these laws : in so far as we are intellectual we incline to regard facts mainly as material for arriving at descriptions which themselves form the material out of which, by a further intellectual effort, explanations are framed in terms of general laws, which we need to know if we are to be ready for what is going to happen. Now these laws are general laws applying to whole classes of facts of one kind, or another. Facts, therefore, only form material for discovering laws in so far as they can be classified into kinds.

The first step in classifying a fact is called analysis and consists in discovering common qualities which the fact possesses. According to Bergson the discovery of common qualities in a fact consists simply in learning to overlook everything in that fact except the respects in which it can be said to be of the same kind, and so to belong to the same class, as other facts. Far from adding to our direct knowledge, as common sense supposes, he holds that analysis consists in shutting our eyes to the individuality of facts in order to dwell only upon what they have in common with one another. Starting, then, from the wider field of knowledge which he assumes Bergson explains how we reach the limited facts, which are all that we ordinarily know, by saying that these facts are arrived at by selection out of this much wider field. It is not the disinterested love of knowledge that determines how much we shall actually attend to: our selection from the whole field of what facts we will attend to is determined by the pressing need of being prepared in advance for the facts which are to come. We attend only to so much of the whole of what is, in some sense, directly known to us as will be useful for framing the general laws which enable us to prepare in advance for what is coming. This practical utility explains why analysis and classification seem to us to be the obvious way of dealing with what we know.

The work of abstraction by which, treating the facts directly known as so much material for framing explanations, we pass from these actual facts to the general laws which explain them, falls into four stages, and at each stage, according to Bergson, as we go further and further from the original fact directly known, the two vices of the intellectual method, limitation and distortion of the actual fact, become more and more apparent.

Starting from the fact directly known, the first thing, as we have seen, is to learn to distinguish common qualities which it shares in common with some, but not all, other facts; the next thing is to classify it by fitting it into the further groups to which these various qualities entitle it to belong. The moment a quality has been distinguished in a fact that fact has been fitted into a class, the class which consists of all the facts in which that quality can be distinguished. Thus, in our original illustration, when you first distinguished warmth, etc., you were beginning to fit your fact into classes: when you perceived warmth you fitted it into the class of warm objects, and it was the same with the other qualities of roughness, size and smell. This fitting of facts into classes according to the common qualities distinguished in them might be called a preliminary classification, but we shall use the term analysis for this preliminary grouping of facts according to their qualities, keeping the term classification for the next step, which you took when you realized "this is a dog," which consists in the discovery not of mere disconnected qualities but of "real things." Just as every quality, such as "warm" or "hairy" or "sweet" or "cold" is a class of actual facts, so every "real thing" such as "a dog" or "an ice cream" is a class of qualities. Thus a quality is once, and a "real thing" is twice, removed from actual fact, and the more energetically we pursue the intellectual work of abstraction the further we get from the fact itself from which we began. The point of grouping facts into classes, whether by analysing them into qualities or classifying them into "real things," is that we can then apply to the particular fact all that we know to be true in general of whatever belongs to these various classes: in a word, once we have fitted a fact into a class we can apply to it all the general laws which are known to apply to that class.

Common sense, as we saw, tells us that when we distinguish qualities in any given fact we obtain fuller knowledge than was given in the mere unanalysed fact, and this knowledge is supposed to become fuller still when we go on to classify these qualities into "real things." Bergson, on the contrary, says that common qualities are arrived at by leaving out much of the fact originally known, while each successive stage in the process of abstraction by which we explain facts, though it enables us to apply more and more general laws, yet leaves out more and more of the actual fact itself. Analysis begins this whittling away of the actual fact by confining our attention to qualities which do not exhaust the whole content of the actual fact. At this preliminary stage, however, though we concentrate our attention on the quality, we still remain aware of the whole fact in which the quality has its setting. Classification carries the work of limitation a stage further. "Things" are a stage further removed from actual fact than qualities are since, while qualities are classes of facts, "things" are only classes of qualities. For classification into "things" therefore only the qualities in a fact will be of any use, and so, when we have reached the stage of classification, we need no longer burden our attention with the actual facts themselves in their entirety, we need pay attention only to the qualities which distinguish one group from another, For the purpose of classification into "things" the quality can stand for the whole fact: thus, as Bergson points out, we begin to lose contact with the whole fact originally known, since all the rest of it except the respects in which it can be analysed will henceforth tend to be ignored.

The third stage in explaining facts in terms of general laws is called induction and consists in observing and formulating the relations of "things." "Things" are related to each other through their qualities. Qualities do not give us the whole fact, because, when we have distinguished qualities, we are inclined to concentrate our attention on the quality at the expense of the rest of the fact; nevertheless while we attend to actual qualities we have not lost contact with fact altogether. Induction, which consists in framing general laws of the relations of "things," though it does not involve attention to the whole fact, does at least demand attention to qualities, and so, while we are occupied with induction, we do still keep touch with fact to some extent.

Once the relations of qualities have been observed and formulated, however, we need no longer attend to any part of the fact at all. Instead of the actual qualities we now take symbols, words, for example, or letters, or other signs, and with these symbols we make for ourselves diagrams of the relations in which we have observed that the qualities which they represent have stood to each other. Thus we might use the words "lightning before thunder" or first an L and then a T, to express the fact that in a storm we usually observe the quality of flashing before the quality of rumbling. Such laws do not actually reveal new facts to us, they can only tell us, provided we actually know a fact belonging to a given class, to what other class facts which we shall know bye and bye will belong. Thus, once we have classified facts as belonging to two classes, daylight and darkness, and have observed the invariable alternation of facts belonging to these classes, then, whenever we know directly facts which can be classed as daylight, we can predict, according to our law of the alternation of the two classes, that bye and bye these facts will give place to others which can be classed as darkness and that bye and bye these in their turn will be replaced by facts which can again be classed as daylight. The practical value of being able to make even such elementary predictions as these is obviously enormous, and this value increases as applied science, which is built up simply by the formulation of more and more comprehensive general laws of this type, widens the field of facts which can be explained. Once the laws are known, moreover, we are able to say to what class the facts must have belonged which preceded a fact of any given class just as easily as we can say to what class the facts which are to follow it will belong. Thus, given a fact which can be classed as daylight, we can infer, by means of the law of the alternation of the classes daylight and darkness, not only that facts which can be classed as darkness will follow bye and bye, but also that facts of that class must have gone before. In this way we can explain the causes of all classifiable facts equally with their effects and so bridge over the gaps in our direct knowledge by creating a unified plan of the interrelations of all the classes to which facts can belong. By means of this plan we can explain any fact (that is classify its causes and effects), provided we can fit it into one or other of the known classes. This again is of enormous practical use because, when we know to what class present facts must belong if they are to be followed by the class of facts which we want, or not to be followed by those which we do not want, we can arrange our present facts accordingly.

Bergson would not think of denying that this intellectual method, in which facts are used as material for abstraction, is of the utmost practical use for explaining facts and so enabling us to control them. He suggests, however, that our preoccupation with these useful abstractions, classes and their relations, misleads us as to the facts themselves. What actually takes place, he thinks, is a kind of substitution of the explanation for the fact which was to be explained, analogous with what happens when a child at a party, or a guest at dinner, is misled about his actual sensations, only this substitution of which Bergson speaks, being habitual, is much harder to see through. Explanation, as we have seen, consists in constructing a plan or map in terms of such abstractions as classes and their relations, or sometimes, when the abstraction has been carried a step further, in terms simply of words or symbols, by means of which we represent the causal relations between such of the actual directly known facts as can be classified. This plan is more comprehensive and complete than the actual facts which we know directly in the ordinary course of things, for which it stands, and it enables us to explain these facts in terms of the classes of causes from which they follow, and the classes of effects which they produce. No explanation, of course, can actually acquaint us directly with the real antecedent or consequent facts themselves : it can only tell us to what classes these facts must belong. The terms of the plan by which we explain the facts, the classes, for instance, daylight and darkness, and their relation of alternation, or the words or symbols which stand for classes and relations are not themselves facts but abstractions. We cannot think in terms of actual facts : the intellectual activity by which we formulate general laws can only work among abstractions, and in order to explain a fact we are obliged to substitute for it either a class or word or other symbol. All description and explanation of facts consists in substitutions of this kind. The explanation applies provided the abstraction is based on fact, that is, provided it is possible to fit the fact to which the explanation is intended to apply into the class employed to explain it : the general law, for instance, about the alternation of the classes daylight and darkness will explain any facts which can be fitted into one or other of these classes, or again general laws about dogs, such as "dogs lick" will apply to whatever fact belongs at once to all the simpler classes, "warm," "rough," "of a certain size, and smell," out of which the class "dog" is constructed. The general law itself, however, does not consist of such facts but of abstractions substituted for the facts themselves. Such substitution is extremely useful and perfectly legitimate so long as we keep firm hold of the fact as well, and are quite clear about what is fact and what only symbol. The danger is, however, that, being preoccupied with describing and explaining and having used abstractions so successfully for these purposes, we may come to lose our sense of fact altogether and fail to distinguish between actual facts and the symbols which we use to explain them.

This, indeed, is just what Bergson thinks really does happen. No doubt an intelligent physicist is perfectly aware that the vibrations and wave lengths and electrons and forces by which he explains the changes that take place in the material world are fictions, and does not confuse them with the actual facts in which his actual knowledge of the material world consists. But it is much more doubtful whether he distinguishes between these actual facts and the common sense material objects, such as lumps of lead, pieces of wood, and so on, which he probably believes he knows directly but which are really only abstractions derived from the facts in order to explain them just as much as his own vibrations and wave lengths. When a scientist frames a hypothesis he employs the intellectual method of substitution with full consciousness of what he is about; he recognises that its terms are abstractions and not facts. But the intellectual method of explaining by substituting general abstractions for particular facts is not confined to science. All description and explanation, from the first uncritical assumptions of common sense right up to the latest scientific hypothesis employs the intellectual method of substituting abstractions for actual facts. The common sense world of things, events, qualities, minds, feelings, and so on, in which we all pass our every day lives is an early and somewhat crude attempt to describe the continually changing fact which each of us experiences directly, but it is perhaps more misleading than the later elaborate constructions of chemistry, physics, biology or physchology in that things and qualities are more easily mistaken for facts than more obviously hypothetical assumptions. Bergson points out that the various things of which this common sense world consists, solid tables, green grass, anger, hope, etc., are not facts: these things, he insists, are only abstractions. They are convenient for enabling us to describe and explain the actual facts which each of us experiences directly, and they are based upon these facts in the sense of being abstracted from them. The objection to them is that we are too much inclined to take it for granted that these things and qualities and events actually are facts themselves, and in so doing to lose sight of the real facts altogether. In support of his view that things having qualities in successive relations are mere abstractions Bergson points out that whenever we stop to examine what it actually is that we know directly we can see at once that this fact does not consist of things and qualities at all: things and qualities are clearly marked off one from another,; they change as a series of distinct terms, but in what we know directly there are no clear cut distinctions and so no series. The assumption which we usually make that the facts must consist of such things as events and qualities and material objects is not based upon the evidence of direct knowledge: we make the assumption that the facts must be of this kind simply because they can be explained in these terms.

It is true that there is some correspondence between the actual facts and the common sense world of solid tables and so on, and we usually jump to the conclusion that this correspondence would not be possible unless the facts had common qualities. There is no denying that facts can be classified and it seems only natural to take it for granted that whatever can be classified must share some quality with whatever belongs to the same class, that, indeed, it is just on account of all sharing the same common quality that facts can be classified as being all of the same kind. Thus common sense takes it for granted that all facts which can be classified as red, and so explained by all the general laws which we know about the relation of red things to other things, must share a common quality of redness. It seems only natural to make this assumption because we are so used to making it, but if we stop to examine the facts which we know directly we discover that they do not bear it out, and we are gradually driven to the conclusion that it is quite unwarranted. It is only bit by bit, as we gradually accustom ourselves to doubting what we have been accustomed to take for granted, that we realize how ill this assumption fits the facts.

CHAPTER II

FACT

COMMON sense starts out with the assumption that what we know directly is such things as trees, grass, anger, hope and so on, and that these things have qualities such as solidity, greenness, unpleasantness and so on, which are also facts directly known. It is not very difficult to show that, if we examine the facts which we know directly, we cannot find in them any such things as trees, grass, or minds, over and above the various qualities which we say belong to them. I see one colour and you see another: both of them are colours belonging to the grass but neither of us can find anything among the facts known to him corresponding to this grass, regarded as something over and above its various qualities, to which those qualities are supposed to belong.

This drives common sense back unto its second line of defence where it takes up the much stronger position of asserting that, while trees, grass, minds, etc., are not among the facts directly known, their qualities of solidity, greenness, etc., are. It is usual to add that these qualities are signs of real trees, grass, etc., which exist independently but are only known to us through their qualities.

It is much harder to attack this position, but its weakness is best exposed by considering change as we know it directly, and comparing this with change as represented in terms of qualities. Change, when represented in terms of qualities, forms a series in which different qualities are strung together one after the other by the aid of temporal relations of before and after. The change perceived when we look at the spectrum would thus have to be described in terms of a series of colours, red before orange, orange before yellow, yellow before green, and so on. We might certainly go into greater detail than this, distinguishing any number of shades in each of the colours mentioned, but the description would still have to be given in the same form, that of a series of different colours, or shades of colour, strung together by relations of before and after. Now the fact which we know directly does not change so: it forms a continuous becoming which is not made up of any number, however great, of fixed stages. When we want to represent this changing fact in terms of qualities we have to put together a series of qualities, such as red, orange, etc., and then say that "the colour" changes from one of these to another. We pretend that there is "a colour" which is not itself either red or green or orange or blue, which changes into all these different colours one after another. It is not very difficult to see that this abstract colour which is neither red nor orange nor green nor blue is not a fact but only an abstraction which is convenient for purposes of description: it is not quite so easy to see that this criticism applies equally to each of the separate colours, red, orange, etc., and yet a little attention shows that these also are really nothing but abstractions. With reference to the whole changing fact which is known directly through any period the change in respect of colour is clearly an abstraction. But just as there is no "colour" over and above the red, the orange, the green, etc., which we say we see, so there is really no "red," "orange," "green," over and above the changing process with which we are directly acquainted. Each of these, the red, the orange, and so on, just like the abstract "colour," is simply a fictitious stage in the process of changing which it is convenient to abstract when we want to describe the process but which does not itself occur as a distinct part in the actual fact.

Change, as we know it directly, does not go on between fixed points such as these stages which we abstract, it goes on impartially, as it were, through the supposed stages just as much as in between them. But though fixed stages are not needed to enable change to occur, simply as a fact, they are needed if we are to describe change and explain it in terms of general laws. Qualities are assumptions required, not in order that change may take place, but in order that we may describe, explain, and so control it. Such particular qualities as red and green are really no more facts directly known than such still more general, and so more obviously fictitious notions as a colour which is of no particular shade, or a table, or a mind, apart from its qualities or states. All these fixed things are alike abstractions required for explaining facts directly known but not occurring as actual parts of those facts or stages in their change.

Thus it appears that the common sense world of things and qualities and events is in the same position, with regard to the actual facts directly known as scientific hypotheses such as forces, electrons, and so on, in their various relations: none of these actually form parts of the fact, all of them are abstractions from the fact itself which are useful for explaining and so controlling it. Common sense stops short at things and qualities and events; science carries the abstraction further, that is all the difference: the aim in both cases is the same, the practical one of explaining and so controlling facts directly known. In both cases the method employed is the intellectual method of abstraction which begins by discriminating within the whole field directly known in favour of just so much as will enable us to classify it and ignoring the rest, and then proceeds to confuse even this selected amount of the actual fact with the abstract classes or other symbols in terms of which it is explained. We have just seen how the result, the worlds of common sense or science, differ from the actual facts in the way in which they change: these worlds of abstractions represent change as a series of fixed stages united by temporal relations, while the actual fact forms a continuous process of becoming which does not contain any such fixed points, as stages in relations.

The more we shake ourselves free from the common sense and scientific bias towards substituting explanations for actual facts the more clearly we see that this continuous process of changing is the very essence of what we know directly, and the more we realize how unlike such a continuous process is to any series of stages in relation of succession.

The unsatisfactoriness of such descriptions is no new discovery: the logical difficulties connected with the attempt to describe change in terms of series of successive things or events have been familiar since the time when Zeno invented the famous dilemma of Achilles' race with the tortoise. Mathematicians have been in the habit of telling us that these difficulties depend simply on the fact that we imagine the series of positions at which Achilles and the tortoise find themselves from moment to moment as finite: the device of the infinite series, they say, satisfies all the requirements needed for representing change and solves all the logical difficulties which arise from it. Bergson's difficulties, however, cannot be solved in this way for they are not based upon the discovery of logical absurdities but upon the discrepancy between the description and the fact. What he maintains is that the description of change in terms of an infinite series of stages leaves out the change altogether. Zeno's logical dilemma as to how Achilles could ever catch up with the tortoise provided the tortoise was given a start, however small, may be countered by the ingenuity of the mathematicians' infinite series. Bergson's difficulty turns on a question of fact, not of logic, and cannot be so met. He solves the problem simply by denying that Achilles or the tortoise ever are at particular points at particular moments. Such a description of change, he says, leaves out the real changing. And the introduction of the notion of an infinite series only makes the matter worse. For stages do not change, and so, if there is to be any change, it must, presumably, take place in between one stage and the next. But in between any two stages of an infinite series there are supposed to be an infinite number of other stages, so that to any given stage there *is* no next stage. Change, therefore, cannot take place between one stage and the next one, there being no next one, and since it is equally impossible that it should take place at any one of the stages themselves it follows that an infinite series of stages leaves out change altogether. Similarly a series of instants before and after one another leaves out of time just the element of passage, becoming, which is its essence.

The truth, Bergson says, is that with fixed stages, no matter how many you take, and no matter in what relation you arrange them, you cannot reproduce the change and time which actually occur as facts directly known. If Achilles or the tortoise are ever at different places at different moments then neither of them really moves at all. Change and time, as represented by abstractions, according to the intellectual method, consist of stages in relations of succession, but the fact does not happen by stages and is not held together by relations: if we compare the representation with the fact we find that they differ profoundly in their form.

According to Bergson this difference in form is one of the two essential respects in which abstractions fail to represent facts and in which, consequently, we are led into error as to the facts if we fail to distinguish them from the abstractions in terms of which we explain them, or take for granted that they correspond exactly with our explanations.

Bergson gives the name "space" to the form which belongs to abstractions but not to actual facts: abstractions, he says, are "spatial," but facts are not. This use of the word "space" is peculiar and perhaps unfortunate. Even as it is ordinarily used the word "space" is ambiguous, it may mean either the pure space with which higher mathematics is concerned, or the public space which contains the common sense things and objects and their qualities which make up the every day world, or the private space of sensible perception. When Bergson speaks of "space," however, he does not mean either pure or public or private space, he means an *a priori* form imposed by intellectual activity upon its object. This resembles Kant's use of the word, but Bergson's "space" is not, like Kant's, the *a priori* form of sense acquaintance, but of thought, in other words logical form. For Bergson "spatial" means "logical," and since so much misunderstanding seems to have been caused by his using the word "space" in this peculiar sense we shall perhaps do better in what follows to use the word "logical" instead.

Now whatever is logical is characterised by

consisting of distinct, mutually exclusive terms in external relations: all schemes, for instance, and diagrams, such as a series of dots one above the other, or one below the other, or one behind, or in front of the other, or a series of instants one after the other, or a series of numbers, or again any arrangements of things or qualities according to their relations, such as colours or sounds arranged according to their resemblance or difference; in all these each dot or instant or number or colour-shade or note, is quite distinct from all the others, and the relations which join it to the others and give it its position in the whole series are external to it in the sense that if you changed its position or included it in quite another series it would nevertheless still be just the same dot or instant or number or quality as before.

These two logical characteristics of mutual distinction of terms and externality of relations certainly do belong to the abstractions employed in explanations, and we commonly suppose that they belong to everything else besides. Bergson, however, believes that these logical characteristics really only belong to abstractions and are not discovered in facts but are imposed upon them by our intellectual bias, in the sense that we take it for granted that the facts which we know directly must have the same form as the abstractions which serve to explain them.

This habit of taking it for granted that not only our abstractions but also the actual facts have the logical characteristics of consisting of mutually exclusive terms joined by external relations is, according to Bergson, one of the two serious respects in which our intellectual bias distorts our direct acquaintance with actual fact. He points out, as we saw, that the facts with which we are acquainted are in constant process of changing, and that, when we examine carefully what is actually going on, we discover that this change does not really form a series of distinct qualities or percepts or states, united by external relations of time, resemblance, difference, and so on, but a continuous process which has what we might call a qualitative flavour but in which distinct qualities, states and so on do not occur.

" Considered in themselves " he says, " profound states of consciousness have no relation to quantity: they are mingled in such a way that it is impossible to say whether they are one or many, or indeed to examine them from that point of view without distorting them." Now, strictly speaking, of course, these " states of consciousness " ought not to be referred to in the plural, it is, in fact, a contradiction to speak of " states of consciousness " having " no relation to quantity " : a plurality must always form some quantity. This contradiction is the natural consequence of attempting to put what is non-logical into words. It would have been just as bad to have referred to "the state of consciousness," in the singular, while at the same time insisting that it contained resemblance and difference. The fact is that plurality and unity, like distinct terms and external relations, apply only to whatever has logical form, and Bergson's whole point is to deny that the fact (or facts) directly known have this form, and so that any of these notions apply to it (or them.)

This, of course, raises difficulties when we try to describe the facts in words, since words stand for abstractions and carry their logical implications. All descriptions in words of what is non-logical are bound to be a mass of contradictions, for, having applied any word it is necessary immediately to guard against its logical implications by adding another which contradicts them. Thus we say our experience is of facts, and must then hastily add that nevertheless they are not plural, and we must further qualify this statement by adding that neither are they singular. A description of what is non-logical can only convey its meaning if we discount all the logical implications of the words which, for want of a better medium of expression, we are driven to employ. Our whole intellectual bias urges us towards describing everything that comes within our experience, even if the description is only for our own private benefit

Unfortunately the language in which these descriptions have to be expressed is so full of logical implications that, unless we are constantly on our guard, we are liable to be carried away by them, and then, at once, we lose contact with the actual facts.

In order to get round this almost universal tendency to confuse abstractions with facts Bergson sometimes tries to get us to see the facts as they actually are by using metaphor instead of description in terms of abstract general notions. He has been much criticised for this but there is really a good deal to be said for attempting to convey facts by substituting metaphors for them rather than by using the ordinary intellectual method of substituting abstractions reached by analysis. Those who have criticised the use of metaphor have for the most part not realized how little removed such description is from the ordinary intellectual method of analysis. They have supposed that in analysis we stick to the fact itself, whereas in using metaphor we substitute for the fact to be described some quite different fact which is only connected with it by a more or less remote analogy. If Bergson's view of the intellectual method is right, however, when we describe in abstract terms arrived at by analysis we are not sticking to the facts at all, we are substituting something else for them just as much as if we were using an out and out metaphor. Qualities and all abstract general notions are, indeed, nothing but marks of analogies between a given fact and all the other facts belonging to the same class: they may mark rather closer analogies than those brought out by an ordinary metaphor, but on the other hand in a frank metaphor we at least stick to the concrete, we substitute fact for fact and we are in no danger of confusing the fact introduced by the metaphor with the actual fact to which the metaphor applies. In description in terms of abstract general notions such as common qualities we substitute for fact something which is not fact at all, we lose touch with the concrete and, moreover, we are strongly tempted to confuse fact with abstraction and believe that the implications of the abstraction apply to the fact, or even that the abstraction is itself a real part of the fact.

Language plays a most important part in forming our habit of treating all facts as material for generalisation, and it is largely to the influence of the words which we use for describing facts that Bergson attributes our readiness to take it for granted that facts have the same logical form as abstractions. It is language again which makes it so difficult to point out that this assumption is mistaken, because, actually, the form of facts is non-logical, a continuous process and not a series. The only way to point this out is by describing the nature of the non-logical facts as contrasted with a logical series, but the language in which our description of the non-logical facts has to be conveyed is itself full of logical implications which contradict the very point we are trying to bring out. Descriptions of non-logical processes will only be intelligible if we discount the logical implications inherent in the words employed, but in order to be willing to discount these implications it is necessary first to be convinced that there is anything non-logical to which such a description could apply. And yet how can we be convinced without first understanding the description ? It appears to be a vicious circle, and so it would be if our knowledge of change as a process really depended upon our understanding anybody's description of it. According to Bergson, however, we all do know such a process directly ; in fact, if he is right, we know nothing else directly at all. The use of description is not to give us knowledge of the process, that we already have, but only to remind us of what we really knew all along, but had rather lost contact with and misinterpreted because of our preoccupation with describing and explaining it. Bergson's criticism of our intellectual methods turns simply upon a question of fact, to be settled by direct introspection. If, when we have freed ourselves from the preconceptions created by our normal common sense intellectual point of view, we find that what we know directly is a non-logical process of becoming, then we must admit that intellectual thinking is altogether inappropriate and even mischievous as a method of speculation.

It is one of Bergson's chief aims to induce us to regain contact with our direct experience, and it is with this in view that he spends so much effort in describing what the form of this experience actually is, and how it compares with the logical form which belongs to abstractions, that is with what he calls "space."

The form which belongs to facts but not to abstractions Bergson calls "duration." Duration can be described negatively by saying that it is non-logical, but when we attempt any positive description language simply breaks down and we can do nothing but contradict ourselves. Duration does not contain parts united by external relations: it does not contain parts at all, for parts would constitute fixed stages, whereas duration changes continuously.

But in order to describe duration at all we have logically only two alternatives, either to speak of it as a plurality, and that implies having parts, or else as a unity, and that by implication, excludes change. Being particularly concerned to emphasise the changing nature of what we know directly

Bergson rejects the latter alternative: short of simply giving up the attempt to describe it he has then no choice but to treat this process which he calls duration as a plurality and this drives him into speaking of it as if it had parts. To correct this false impression he adds that these parts are united, not, like logical parts, by external relations, but in quite a new way, by "synthesis." "Parts" united by synthesis have not the logical characteristics of mutual distinction and externality of relations, they interpenetrate and modify one another. In a series which has duration (such a thing is a contradiction in terms, but the fault lies with the logical form of language which, in spite of its unsatisfactoriness we are driven to employ if we want to describe at all) the "later parts" are not distinct from the "earlier": "earlier and" "later" are not mutually exclusive relations.

Bergson says, then, that the process of duration which we know directly, if it is to be called a series at all, must be described as a series whose "parts" interpenetrate, and this is the first important respect in which non-logical duration differs from a logical series. In "a series" which is used to describe duration not only are the "parts" not distinct but "their relations" are not external in the sense, previously explained, in which logical relations are external to the terms which they relate. A logical term in a logical series can change its position or enter into a wholly different series and still remain the same term. But the terms in a series which has duration (again this is absurd) are what they are just because of their position in the whole stream of duration to which they belong: to transfer them from one position in the series to another would be to alter their whole flavour which depends upon having had just that particular past and no other. As illustration we might take the last bar of a tune. By itself, or following upon other sounds not belonging to the tune, this last bar would not be itself, its particular quality depends upon coming at the end of that particular tune. In a process of duration, then, such as tune, the "later" bars are not related externally to the "earlier" but depend for their character upon their position in the whole tune. In actual fact, of course, the tune progresses continuously, and not by stages, such as distinct notes or bars, but if, for the sake of description, we speak of it as composed of different bars, we must say that any bar we choose to distinguish is modified by the whole of the tune which has gone before it: change its position in the whole stream of sound to which it belongs and you change its character absolutely.

This means that in change such as this, change, that is, which has duration, repetition is out of the question. Take a song in which the last line is sung twice over as a refrain: the notes, we say, are repeated, but the second time the line occurs the actual effect produced is different, and that, indeed, is the whole point of a refrain. This illustrates the second important difference which Bergson wants to bring out between the forms of change which belong respectively to non-logical facts and to the logical abstractions by which we describe them, that is between duration as contrasted with a logical series of stages. The notes are abstractions assumed to explain the effect produced, which is the actual fact directly known. The notes are stages in a logical series of change, but their effects, the actual fact, changes as a process of duration. From this difference in their ways of changing there follows an important difference between fact and abstraction, namely that, while the notes can be repeated over again, the effect will never be the same as before. This is because the notes, being abstractions, are not affected by their relations which give them their position in the logical series which they form, while their effect, being a changing process, depends for its flavour upon its position in the whole duration to which it belongs: this flavour grows out of the whole of what has gone before, and since this whole is itself always growing by the addition of more and more " later stages," the effect which it goes to produce can never be the same twice over.

This is why Bergson calls duration "creative."

No " two " positions in a creative process of duration can have an identical past history, every " later " one will have more history, every " earlier " one less. In a logical series, on the other hand, there is no reason why the same term should not occur over and over again at different points in the course of the series, since in a logical series every term, being distinct from every other and only joined to it by external relations, is what it is independently of its position.

If Bergson is right therefore in saying that abstractions change as a logical series while the actual facts change as a creative process of duration, it follows that, while our descriptions and explanations may contain repetitions the actual fact to which we intend these explanations to apply, cannot. This, if true, is a very important difference between facts and abstractions which common sense entirely overlooks when it assumes that we are directly acquainted with common qualities.

We have seen that this assumption is taken for granted in the account which is ordinarily given (or would be given if people were in the habit of putting their common sense assumptions into words) of how it is that facts come to be classified: facts are supposed to fall into classes because they share common qualities, that is because, in the changing fact directly known, the same qualities recur over and over again. There is no doubt that the fact with which we are directly acquainted can be classified, and it is equally undeniable that this fact is always changing, but if this change has the form of creative duration then its classification cannot be based upon the repetition of qualities at different "stages" in its course. It follows that either the fact with which we are directly acquainted does not change as a creative process, or else that we are quite wrong in assuming, as we ordinarily do, that we actually know qualities directly and that it is these qualities which form the basis of classification, and hence of all description and explanation. We have already seen that this assumption, though at first sight one naturally supposes it to be based on direct acquaintance, may really depend not on any fact directly known but on our preoccupation with explanation rather than with mere knowing.

But if we never really are acquainted with qualities, if qualities are, as Bergson says, mere abstractions, how come we to be able to make these abstractions, and why do they apply to actual facts? If classification is not based on common qualities discovered by analysis and repeated over and over as actual facts directly known, on what is it based? We certainly can classify facts and these abstract common qualities, if abstractions they be, certainly correspond to something in the facts since they apply to them: what is the foundation in directly knowu fact which accounts for this correspondence between abstractions and facts if it is not qualities actually given as part of the facts? These questions are so very pertinent and at the same time so difficult to answer satisfactorily that one is tempted to throw over the view that the changing fact which we know directly forms a creative duration. This view is impossible to express without self-contradiction and it does not fit in with our accustomed habits of mind: nevertheless if we do not simply reject it at once as patently absurd but keep it in mind for a while and allow ourselves time to get used to it, it grows steadily more and more convincing: we become less and less able to evade these difficult questions by accepting the common sense account of what we know directly as consisting of a series of qualities which are repeated over and over, and more and more driven to regard it as a process in creative duration which does not admit of repetitions. There is no difficulty in seeing, the moment we pay attention, that what we know directly certainly does change all the time: but if we try to pin this change down and hold it so as to examine it we find it slipping through our fingers, and the more we look into the supposed stages, such as things and qualities and events, by means of which common sense assumes that this change takes place, the more it becomes apparent that these stages are all of them mere arbitrary abstractions dragged from their context in a continuous process, fictitious halting places in a stream of change which goes on unbroken. Unbiassed attention to the actual fact cannot fail to convince us that what we know directly changes as a process and not by a series of stages.

The creativeness of this process is perhaps at first not quite so obvious, but if we look into the fact once more, with the object of observing repetitions in it, we realize that we cannot find any. It is true that you can pick out qualities which at first appear to recur : you may, for example, see a rose and then a strawberry ice cream, and you may be inclined to say that here you saw the quality pink twice over. But you can only say that what you saw was the same both times by abstracting what we call the colour from the whole context in which it actually appeared on the two different occasions. In reality the colour is not known in isolation : it has its place, in the whole changing fact in a particular context which you may describe in abstract terms as consisting of the shape and smell and size of the object together with all the rest of your state of mind at the moment, which were not the same on the two different occasions, while further this pink colour was modified on each occasion by its position in the whole changing fact which may again be described in abstract terms by saying, for instance, that the pink on the occasion of your seeing the strawberry ice cream, coming after the pink on the occasion of your seeing the rose, had a peculiar flavour of " seen before " which was absent on the previous occasion. Thus although, by isolating " parts " of the whole process of changing which you know directly, you may bring yourself for a moment to suppose that you are acquainted with repetitions, when you look at the whole fact as it actually is, you see that what you know is never the same twice over, and that your direct experience forms, not a series of repetitions, but a creative process.

But, once you grant that the fact which you know directly really changes, there is, according to Bergson, no getting away from the conclusion that it must form a creative process of duration. For he thinks that creative duration is the only possible way in which the transition between past and present, which is the essential feature of change and time, could be accomplished : all passing from past to present, all change, therefore, and all time, *must*, he says, form a creative process of duration. The alternative is to suppose that time and change form logical series of events in temporal relations of before and after, but, according to Bergson, this not only leaves out the transition altogether but is, even as it stands, unintelligible. The argument is this.

If time and change are real, then, when the present is, the past simply is not. But it is impossible to see how, in that case, there can be any relation between past and present, for a relation requires at least two terms in between which it holds, while in this case there could never be more than one term, the present, *ipso facto*, abolishing the past. If, on the other hand, the past is preserved, distinct from the present, then temporal relations can indeed hold between them, but in that case there is no real change nor time at all.

This dilemma all follows, of course, from regarding "past" and "present" as mutually exclusive and distinct, and requiring to be united by external relations, in short as terms in a logical series: for Bergson himself this difficulty simply does not arise since he denies that, within the actual changing fact directly known, there are any clear cut logical distinctions such as the words "past" and "present" imply. But when it comes to describing this changing fact distinct terms have to be employed because there are no others, and this creates pseudo-problems such as this question of how, assuming past and present to be distinct, the transition between them ever can be effected. The real answer is that the transition never is effected because past and present are, in fact, not distinct.

According to Bergson a very large proportion of the problems over which philosophers have been accustomed to dispute have really been pseudo-problems simply arising out of this confusion between facts and the abstractions by which we describe them. When once we have realized how they arise these pseudo-problems no longer present any difficulties; they are in fact no longer problems at all, they melt away and cease to interest us. If Bergson is right this would go far to explain the suspicion which, in spite of the prestige of philosophy, still half unconsciously colours the feeling of the "plain man" for the "intellectual," and which even haunts the philosopher himself, in moments of discouragement, the suspicion that the whole thing is trivial, a dispute about words of no real importance or dignity. If Bergson is right this suspicion is, in many cases, all too well founded: the discussion of pseudo-problems is not worth while. But then the discussion of pseudo-problems is not real philosophy: the thinker who allows himself to be entangled in pseudo-problems has lost his way.

In this, however, the "intellectuals" are not the only ones at fault. "Plain men" are misled by abstractions about facts just as much, only being less thorough, their mistake has less effect : at the expense of a little logical looseness their natural sense of fact saves them from all the absurdities which follow from their false assumptions. For the "intellectual" there is not this loophole through which the sense of fact may undo some of the work of false assumptions : the "intellectual" follows out ruthlessly the implications of his original assumptions and if these are false his very virtues lead him into greater absurdities than those committed by "plain men."

One of the most important tasks of philosophy is to show up the pseudo-problems so that they may no longer waste our time and we may be free to pursue the real aim of philosophy which is the reconquest of the field of virtual knowledge. Getting rid of the pseudo-problems, however, is no easy task : we may realize, for example, that the difficulty of seeing how the transition between past and present ever can be effected is a pseudo-problem because in fact past and present are not distinct and so no transition between them is needed. But since we have constantly to be using words which carry the implication of distinctness we are constantly liable to forget this simple answer when new problems, though in fact they all spring from this fundamental discrepancy between facts and the abstractions by which we describe them, present themselves in some slightly different form.

The notion of duration as consisting of "parts" united by "creative synthesis" is a device, not for explaining how the transition from past to present really takes place (this does not need explaining since, "past" and "present" being mere abstractions, no transition between them actually takes place at all), but for enabling us to employ the abstractions "past" and "present" without constantly being taken in by their logical implications. The notion of "creative synthesis" as what joins "past" and "present" in a process of duration is an antidote to the logical implications of these two distinct terms: creative synthesis, unlike logical relations, is not external to the "parts" which it joins; "parts" united by creative synthesis are not distinct and mutually exclusive. Such a notion as this of creative synthesis contradicts the logical implications contained in the notion of parts. The notion of "parts" united by "creative synthesis" is really a hybrid which attempts to combine the two incompatible notions of logical distinction and duration. The result is self-contradictory and this contradiction acts as a reminder warning us against confusing the actual changing fact with the abstractions in terms of which we describe it and so falling into the mistake of taking it for granted that this changing fact must form a series of distinct stages or things or events or qualities, which can be repeated over and over again.

At the same time there is no getting away from the fact that this changing fact lends itself to classification and that explanations in terms of abstractions really do apply to it most successfully. We are therefore faced with the necessity of finding some way of accounting for this, other than by assuming that the facts which we know directly consist of qualities which recur over and over again.

CHAPTER III

MATTER AND MEMORY

We have seen that, according to the theory of change which is fundamental for Bergson's philosophy, the changing fact which we know directly is described as a process of becoming which does not contain parts nor admit of repetitions. On the other hand this changing fact certainly does lend itself to analysis and classification and explanation and, at first sight at any rate, it is natural to suppose that whatever can be classified and explained must consist of qualities, that is distinct parts which can be repeated on different occasions. The problem for Bergson, if he is to establish his theory of change, is to show that the fact that a changing process can be analysed and classified does not necessarily imply that such a process must consist of distinct qualities which can be repeated. Bergson's theory of the relation of matter to memory suggests a possible solution of this problem as to how it is possible to analyse and so apply general laws to and explain duration: it becomes necessary, therefore, to give some account of this theory.

Like all other descriptions and explanations, such an account must, of course, be expressed in terms of abstractions, and so is liable to be misunderstood unless the false implications of these abstractions are allowed for and discounted.

According to Bergson the only actual reality is the changing fact itself, everything else is abstraction: this reality however is not confined to the fragment called "our present experience" which is in the full focus of consciousness and is all that we usually suppose ourselves to know directly; it includes besides everything that we are in a sense aware of but do not pay attention to, together with our whole past: for Bergson, in fact, reality coincides with the field of virtual knowledge, anything short of this whole field is an abstraction and so falsified. Even to say "we know this fact" is unsatisfactory as implying ourselves and the fact as distinct things united by an external relation of knowing: to say "the fact is different from the abstraction by which it is explained" similarly implies logically distinct terms in an external relation of difference, and so on. If Bergson is right in claiming that the actual fact is non-logical then obviously all attempts to describe it, since they must be expressed in terms of abstractions, will teem with false implications which must be discounted if the description is to convey the meaning intended.

Bergson's claim is that if we allow ourselves to attend to the changing fact with which we are actually acquainted we are driven to a theory of reality different from the theory of things and relations accepted by common sense. The two abstractions by means of which he attempts to express this new theory are matter and memory. In the actual fact Bergson would hold that both these notions are combined by synthesis in such a way as no longer to be distinct, or rather, for this implies that they started distinct and then became merged, it would perhaps be better to say that these two notions are abstractions from two tendencies which are present in the actual fact. In the actual fact they combine and, as it were, counteract one another and the result is something different from either taken alone, but when we abstract them we release them from each other's modifying influence and the result is an exaggeration of one or other tendency which does not really represent anything which actually occurs but can be used, in combination with the contrary exaggeration, to explain the actual fact which may be described as being like what would result from a combination of these two abstractions.

We will take matter first.

Matter, for Bergson, is an exaggeration of the tendency in reality, (that is in the actual changing fact directly known) towards logical distinctness, what he calls "spatiality." His use of the word "matter" in this sense is again, perhaps, like his use of the word "space," rather misleading. Actual reality, according to him, is never purely material, the only purely material things are abstractions, and these are not real at all but simply fictions. Bergson really means the same thing by "matter" as by "space" and that is simply mutual distinctness of parts and externality of relations, in a word logical complexity. Matter, according to this definition of the word, has no duration and so cannot last through any period of time or change: it simply *is* in the present, it does not endure but is perpetually destroyed and recreated.

The complementary exaggeration which, taken together with matter, completes Bergson's explanation of reality, is memory. Just as matter is absolute logical complexity memory is absolute creative synthesis. Together they constitute the hybrid notion of creative duration whose "parts" interpenetrate which, according to Bergson, comes nearest to giving a satisfactory description of the actual fact directly known which is, for him, the whole reality.

The best way to accustom one's mind to these two complementary exaggerations, matter and memory, and to see in more detail the use that Bergson makes of them in explaining the actual facts, will be to examine his theory of sensible perception, since it is just in the act of sensible perception that memory comes in contact with matter.

The unsophisticated view is that in sensible perception we become acquainted with things which exist whether we perceive them or not, and these things, taken all together, are commonly called the material world. According to Bergson's theory also sensible perception is direct acquaintance with matter. The unsophisticated view holds further, however, that this material world with which sensible perception acquaints us is the common sense world of solid tables, green grass, anger and other such states and things and qualities, but we have already seen that this common sense world is really itself only one among the various attempts which science and common sense are continually making to explain the facts in terms of abstractions. The worlds of electrons, vibrations, forces, and so on, constructed by physics, are other attempts to do the same thing and the common sense world of "real" things and qualities has no more claim to actual existence than have any of these scientific hypotheses. Bergson's matter is not identified with any one of these constructions, it is that in the facts which they are all attempts to explain in terms of abstractions, the element in the facts upon which abstractions are based and which makes facts classifiable and so explicable.

The words by which we describe and explain the material element in the facts in terms of series of distinct stages or events in external relations would leave out change if their implications were followed out consistently, but it is only a few "intellectuals" who have ever been able to bring themselves to follow out this implication to the bitter end and accept the conclusion, however absurd. Since it is obvious that the facts do change the usual way of getting round the difficulty is to say that some of these stages are "past" and some "present," and then, not clearly realizing that the explanations we construct are not really facts at all, to take it for granted that a transition between past and present, though there is no room for it in the logical form of the explanation, yet somehow manages actually to take place. Bergson agrees that change does actually take place but not as a transition between abstractions such as "past" and "present." We think that "past" and "present" must be real facts because we do not realize clearly how these notions have been arrived at. Once we have grasped the idea that these notions, and indeed all clear concepts, are only abstractions, we see that it is not necessary to suppose that these abstractions really change at all. Between the abstractions "the past" and "the present" there is no transition, and it is the same with events and things and qualities: all these, being nothing but convenient fictions, stand outside the stream of actual fact which is what really changes and endures.

Matter, then, is the name which Bergson gives to that element in the fact upon which the purely logical form appropriate to abstractions is based. The actual facts are not purely logical but neither are they completely interpenetrated since they lend themselves to classification: they tend to logical form on the one hand and to complete interpenetration on the other without going the whole way in either direction. What Bergson does in the description of the facts which he offers is to isolate each of these tendencies making them into two separate distinct abstractions, one called matter and the other mind. Isolated, what in the actual fact was blended becomes incompatible. Matter and mind, the clear cut abstractions, are mutually contradictory and it becomes at once a pseudo-problem to see how they ever could combine to constitute the actual fact.

The matter which Bergson talks about, being what would be left of the facts if memory were abstracted, has no past: it simply *is* in the present moment. If there is any memory which can retain previous moments then this memory may compare these previous moments with the present moment and call them the past of matter, but in itself, apart from memory, (and so isolated in a way in which this tendency in the actual fact never could be isolated) matter has no past.

Noticing how very different the actual facts which we know directly are from any of the material worlds by which we explain them, each of which lays claim to being " the reality with which sensible perception acquaints us," some philosophers have put forward the view that in sensible perception we become acquainted, not with matter itself, but with signs which stand for a material world which exists altogether outside perception. This view Bergson rejects. He says that in sensible perception we are not acquainted with mere signs but, in so far as there is any matter at all, what we know in sensible perception is that matter itself. The facts which we know directly are matter itself and would be nothing but matter if they were instantaneous. For Bergson, however, an instantaneous fact is out of the question : every fact contains more than the mere matter presented at the moment of perception. Facts are distinguished from matter by lasting through a period of duration, this is what makes the difference between the actual fact and any of the material worlds in terms of which we describe them : matter, is, as we have said, only an abstraction of one element or tendency in the changing fact which is the sole reality : memory is the complementary abstraction. Apart from the actual fact neither matter nor memory have independent existence. This is where Bergson disagrees with the philosophers who regard the facts as signs of an independent material world, or as phenomena which misrepresent some "thing" in "itself" which is what *really* exists but which is not known directly but only inferred from the phenomena. For Bergson it is the fact directly known that *really* exists, and matter and memory, solid tables, green grass, electrons, forces, the absolute, and all the other abstract ideas by which we explain it are misrepresentations of it, not it of them.

Even Bergson, however, does not get away from the distinction between appearance and reality. The fact is for him the reality, the abstraction the appearance. But then the fact which is the reality is not the fact which we ordinarily suppose ourselves to know, the little fragment which constitutes "our experience at the present moment." This is itself an abstraction from the vastly wider fact of our virtual knowledge, and it is this wider field of knowledge which is the reality. Abstraction involves falsification and so the little fragment of fact to which our attention is usually confined is not, as it stands, reality : it is appearance. We should only know reality as it is if we could replace this fragment in its proper context in the whole field of virtual knowledge (or reality) where it belongs. What we should then know would not be appearance but reality itself. It is at this knowledge, according to Bergson, that philosophy aims. Philosophy is a reversal of our ordinary intellectual habits: ordinarily thought progresses from abstraction to abstraction steadily getting further from concrete facts: according to Bergson the task of philosophy should be to put abstractions back again into their context so as to obtain the fullest possible knowledge of actual fact.

In order to describe and explain this fact, however, we have to make use of abstractions. Bergson describes the fact known directly by sensible perception as a contraction of a period of the duration of matter in which the "past" states of matter are preserved along with the "present" and form a single whole with it. It is memory which makes this difference between matter and the actual facts by preserving "past" matter and combining it with "the present." A single perceived fact, however, does not contain memories as distinct from present material: the distinction between "past" and "present" does not hold inside facts whose duration forms a creative whole and not a logical series. Of course it is incorrect to describe facts as "containing past and present matter," but, as we have often pointed out, misleading though their logical implications are, we are obliged to replace facts by abstractions when we want to describe them.

An example may perhaps convey what is meant by saying that a fact is a contraction of a period of the duration of matter. Consider red, bearing in mind that, when we are speaking of the fact actually perceived when we see red we must discount the logical implications of our words. Science says that red, the material, is composed of immensely rapid vibrations of ether: red, the fact, we know as a simple colour. Bergson accepts the scientific abstractions in terms of which to describe matter, making the reservation that, if we are to talk of matter as composed of vibrations, we must not say that these vibrations last through a period of time or change by themselves, apart from any memory which retains and so preserves the "past" vibrations. If matter is to be thought of at all as existing apart from any memory it must be thought of as consisting of a single vibration in a perpetual present with no past. We might alter the description and say that this present moment of matter should be thought of as being perpetually destroyed and recreated.

Now according to Bergson the red which we know directly *is* a period of the vibrations of matter contracted by memory so as to produce an actual perceived fact. As matter red does not change, it is absolutely discrete and complex, in a word, logical: as fact it is non-logical and forms a creative process of duration. The difference between matter and the actual fact is made by the mental act which holds matter as it were in tension through a period of duration, when a fact is produced, but which would have had to be absent if there had been no fact but simply present matter. Bergson calls this act memory: memory, he says, turns matter into fact by preserving its past along with its present. Without memory there would be no duration and so no change and no time. Matter, apart from memory would have no duration and it is just in this that it is distinguished from actual fact.

It is, however, of course, only by making abstractions that we can say what things would be like if something were taken away which actually is not taken away. Matter never really does exist without memory nor memory without its content, matter: the actual fact can only be described as a combination of the two elements, but this description must not lead us into supposing that the abstractions, matter and memory, actually have independent existence apart from the fact which they explain. Only the actual fact exists and it is not really made up of two elements, matter and memory, but only described in terms of these two abstractions.

Bergson's account of perception differs from the account ordinarily given in that perception is not described as a relation which is supposed to hold between a subject and an object: for Bergson there is no "I," distinct from what is perceived, standing to it in a relation of perception. For an object, to be perceived consists, not in being related to a perceiver, but in being combined in a new way with other objects. If an object is combined by synthesis with other objects then it is perceived and so becomes a fact. But there is no mind over and above the objects which perceives them by being related to them, or even by performing an act of synthesis upon them. To speak of "our" perceiving objects is a mere fiction: when objects are combined by synthesis they become perceptions, facts, and this is the same as saying that they are minds. For Bergson a mind *is* nothing but a synthesis of objects. This explains what he means by saying that in direct knowledge the perceiver is the object perceived.

Actually he thinks such notions as the perceiver and the object and the relation which unites them, or again matter and the act of synthesis which turns matter into fact, are nothing but abstractions: the only thing there really is is simply the fact itself. These abstractions, however, do somehow apply to the actual facts, and this brings us back to our problem as to how it is that the actual fact, which is in creative duration, lends itself to classification : how it is that general laws in terms of abstractions which can be repeated over and over again, can apply to the actual fact which does not contain repetitions ?

Facts lend themselves to explanation when they are perceived as familiar. In this perceived familiarity, which is the basis of all abstraction, and so of all description and explanation, past as well as present is involved, the present owing its familiarity to our memory of past facts. The obvious explanation of perceived familiarity, would be, of course, to say that it results from our perceiving similar qualities shared by past and present facts, or relations of similarity holding between them. But Bergson must find some other explanation than this since he denies that there can be repetition in actual facts directly known.

Whenever there is actual fact there is memory, and memory creates duration which excludes repetition. Perceived familiarity depends upon memory but memory, according to Bergson, does not work by preserving a series of repetitions for future reference. If we say that memory connects " the past " with " the present " we must add that it destroys their logical distinctness. But of course this is putting it very badly: there is really no "logical distinctness" in the actual fact for memory to "destroy": our language suggests that first there was matter, forming a logical series of distinct qualities recurring over and over, and then memory occurred and telescoped the series, squeezing "earlier" and "later" moments into one another to make a creative duration. Such a view is suggested by our strong bias towards regarding abstractions as having independent existence apart from the real fact from which they have been abstracted: if we can overcome this bias the description will do well enough.

According to Bergson, as we have just seen, every actual fact must contain some memory otherwise it would not be a fact but simply matter, since it is an act of memory that turns matter into perceived fact. Our ordinary more or less familiar facts, however, contain much more than this bare minimum. The facts of everyday life are perceived as familiar and classified from a vast number of points of view. When you look at a cherry you recognise its colour, shape, etc., you know it is edible, what it would taste like, whether it is ripe, and much more besides, all at a glance. All this knowledge depends on memory, memory gives meaning to what we might call bare sensation (which is the same thing as

Bergson's present matter) as opposed to the full familiar fact actually experienced. Now the meaning is ordinarily contained in the actual fact along with the bare sensation, not as a multiplicity of memories distinct from the bare sensation, but, as we put it, at a glance. This peculiar flavour of a familiar fact can be analysed out as consisting of memories of this or that past experience, if we choose to treat it in that way, just as a fact can be analysed into qualities. According to Bergson this analysis of the meaning of a familiar fact into memories would have the same drawbacks as the analysis of a present fact into qualities : it would leave out much of the meaning and distort the rest. Bergson holds that wherever there is duration the past must be preserved since it is just the preservation of the past, the creation of fact by a synthesis of what, out of synthesis, would be past and present, which constitutes duration. The essential point about mental life is just the performing of this act of synthesis which makes duration : wherever there is mental life there is duration and so wherever there is mental life the past is preserved. "Above everything," Bergson says, "consciousness signifies memory. At this moment as I discuss with you I pronounce the word "discussion." It is clear that my consciousness grasps this word altogether ; if not it would not see it as a unique word and would not make sense of it. And yet when I pronounce the last syllable of the word the two first ones have already been pronounced; relatively to this one, which must then be called present, they are past. But this last syllable "sion" was not pronounced instantaneously; the time, however short, during which I was saying it, can be split up into parts and these parts are past, relatively to the last of them, and this last one would be present if it were not that it too can be further split up: so that, do what you will, you cannot draw any line of demarcation between past and present, and so between memory and consciousness. Indeed when I pronounce the word "discussion" I have before my mind, not only the beginning, the middle and the end of the word, but also the preceding words, also the whole of the sentence which I have already spoken; if it were not so I should have lost the thread of my speech. Now if the punctuation of the speech had been different my sentence might have begun earlier; it might, for instance, have contained the previous sentence and my "present" would have been still further extended into the past. Let us push this reasoning to its conclusion: let us suppose that my speech has lasted for years, since the first awakening of my consciousness, that it has consisted of a single sentence, and that my consciousness has been sufficiently detached from the future, sufficiently disinterested to occupy itself exclusively in taking in the meaning of the sentence : in that case I should not look for any explanation of the total conservation of this sentence any more than I look for one of the survival of the first two syllables of the word " discussion " when I pronounce the last one. Well, I think that our whole inner life is like a single sentence, begun from the first awakening of consciousness, a sentence scattered with commas, but nowhere broken by a full stop. And so I think that our whole past is there, subconscious—I mean present to us in such a way that our consciousness, to become aware of it, need not go outside itself nor add anything foreign : to perceive clearly all that it contains, or rather all that it is, it has only to put aside an obstacle, to lift a veil. "*

If this theory of memory be correct, the occurrence of any present bare sensation itself suffices to recall, in some sense, the whole past. But this is no use for practical purposes, just as the whole of the fact given in present perception is useless for practical purposes until it has been analysed into qualities. According to Bergson we treat the material supplied by memory in much the same way as that supplied by perception. The whole field of the past which the present calls up is much wider than what we actually remember clearly : what we actually remember is arrived at by ignoring all the past except such scraps as appear to

* *L'Energie Spirituelle*—" L'Ame et le Corps," pages 59 and 60.

form useful precedents for behaviour in the present situation in which we find ourselves. Perhaps this explains why sometimes, at the point of death, when useful behaviour is no longer possible, this selection breaks down and the whole of the past floods back into memory. The brain, according to Bergson, is the organ whose function it is to perform this necessary work of selection out of the whole field of virtual memory of practically useful fragments, and so long as the brain is in order, only these are allowed to come through into consciousness as clear memories. The passage just quoted goes on to speak of "the part played by the brain in memory." "The brain does not serve to preserve the past but primarily to obscure it, and then to let just so much as is practically useful slip through."

But the setting of the whole past, though it is ignored for convenience, still makes itself felt in the peculiar qualitative flavour which belongs to every present fact by reason of its past. Even in the case of familiar facts this flavour is no mere repetition but is perpetually modified as the familiarity increases, and it is just in this progressively changing flavour that their familiarity consists.

An inspection of what we know directly, then, does not bear out the common sense theory that perceived familiarity, upon which abstraction and all description and explanation are based, consists in the perception of similar qualities shared by present matter and the matter retained by memory. A familiar fact appears to be, not a repetition, but a *new* fact. This new fact may be described as containing present and past bare sensations, but it must be added that these bare sensations do not remain distinct things but are synthesised by the act of perception into a fresh whole which is not the sum of the bare sensations which it may be described as containing. Such a perceived whole will be familiar, and so lend itself to abstraction and explanation, in so far as the present bare sensation which it contains, taken as mere matter (that is apart from the act of perception which turns it from mere matter into actual fact), would have been a repetition of some of the past bare sensations which go to form its meaning and combine with it to create the fact actually known. For bare sensation now may be a repetition of past bare sensation though the full fact will always be something fresh, its flavour changing as it grows more and more familiar by taking up into itself more and more bare sensation which, taken in abstraction apart from the act of synthesis which turns it into actual fact, would be repetitions. To take the example which we have already used of perceiving first a rose and then a strawberry ice cream: let us suppose that the rose was the very first occasion on which you saw pink. The perceived fact on that occasion would, like all perceived facts, be a combination of past and present bare sensations. It would not be familiar because the elements of present bare sensation would not be repetitions of the elements of past bare sensation (always assuming, as we must for purposes of explanation, that past and present bare sensations ever could be isolated from the actual fact and still both exist, which, however, is not possible). But when you saw the strawberry ice cream the past perceived rose would be among the memories added to this bare sensation which constitute its meaning and, by forming a synthesis with it, turn it from mere matter into fact. The pink would now be perceived as familiar because the pink of the rose (which as bare sensation is similar to the bare sensation of strawberry-ice-cream-pink) would be included, along with the present bare sensation of pink, in the whole fact of the perception of strawberry ice cream.

Perceived fact, then, combines meaning and present bare sensation to form a whole with a qualitative flavour which is itself always unique, but which lends itself to abstraction in so far as the bare sensations, past and present, which go to produce it, would, as matter in isolation, be repetitions.

This qualitative flavour, however, is, of course, not a quality in the logical sense which implies distinctness and externality of relations. Facts have logical qualities only if they are taken in abstraction isolated from their context. This is not how fact actually occurs. Every fact occurs in the course of the duration of some mental life which itself changes as a process of duration and not as a logical series. The mental life of an individual is, as it were, a comprehensive fact which embraces all the facts directly known to that individual in a single process of creative duration. Facts are to the mental life of an individual what bare sensation is to the actual fact directly known in perception : facts are, as it were, the matter of mental life. Imagine a fact directly known, such as we have described in discussing sensible perception, lasting on and on, perpetually taking up new bare sensations and complicating them with meaning which consists of all the past which it already contains so as to make out of this combination of past and present fresh fact, that will give you some idea of the way in which Bergson thinks that mental life is created out of matter by memory. Only this description is still unsatisfactory because it is obliged to speak of what is created either in the plural or in the singular and so fails to convey either the differentiation contained in mental life or else its unbroken continuity as all one fact progressively modified by absorbing more and more matter.

If Bergson's account of the way in which memory works is true there is a sense in which the whole past of every individual is preserved in memory and all unites with any present bare sensation to constitute the fact directly known to him at any given moment. If the continuity of duration is really unbroken there is no possibility of any of the past being lost.

This is why Bergson maintains that the whole of our past is contained in our virtual knowledge: what he means by our virtual knowledge is simply everything which enters into the process of duration which constitutes our whole mental life. Besides our whole past this virtual knowledge must also contain much more of present bare sensation than we are usually aware of.

We said that, for Bergson, actual fact directly known was the only reality; this actual fact, however, does not mean merely what is present to the perception of a given individual at any given moment, but the whole of our virtual knowledge. The field of virtual knowledge would cover much the same region as the subconscious, which plays such an important part in modern psychology. The limits of this field are impossible to determine. Once you give up limiting direct knowledge to the fact actually present in perception at any given moment it is difficult to draw the line anywhere. And yet to draw the line at the present moment is impossible for "the present moment" is clearly an abstract fiction. For practical purposes "the present" is what is known as "the specious present," which covers a certain ill-defined period of duration from which the instantaneous "present moment" is recognised to be a mere abstraction. According to Bergson, however, just as "the present moment" is only an abstraction from a wider specious present so this specious present itself is an abstraction from a continuous process of duration from which other abstractions, days, weeks, years, can be made, but which is actually unbroken and forms a single continuous changing whole. And just as facts are only abstractions from the whole mental life of an individual so individuals must be regarded as abstractions from some more comprehensive mental whole and thus our virtual knowledge seems not merely to extend over the whole of what is embraced by our individual acts of perception and preserved by our individual memories but overflows even these limits and must be regarded as co-extensive with the duration of the whole of reality.

It may be open to question how much of this virtual knowledge of both past and present we ever could know directly in any sense comparable to the way in which we know the fact actually presented at some given moment, however perfectly we might succeed in ridding ourselves with our intellectual pre-occupation with explaining instead of knowing; but, if reality forms an unbroken whole in duration, we cannot in advance set any limits, short of the whole of reality, to the field of virtual knowledge. And it does really seem as if our pre-occupation with discovering repetitions in the interests of explanation had something to do with the limited extent of the direct knowledge which we ordinarily enjoy, so that, if we could overcome this bias, we might know more than we do now, though how much more it is not possible, in advance, to predict. For in the whole field of virtual knowledge, which appears to be continuous with the little scrap of fact which is all that we usually attend to, present bare sensation and such bare sensations as resemble it, form very insignificant elements: for purposes of abstraction and explanation, however, it is only these insignificant elements that are of any use. So long, therefore, as we are pre-occupied with abstraction, we must bend all our energies towards isolating these fragments from the context which extends out and out over the whole field of virtual knowledge, rivetting our attention on them and, as far as possible, ignoring all the rest. If Bergson's theory of virtual knowledge is correct, then, it does seem as if normally our efforts were directed towards shutting out most of our knowledge rather than towards enjoying it, towards forgetting the greater part of what memory contains rather than towards remembering it.

If we really could reverse this effort and concentrate upon knowing the whole field of past and present as fully as possible, instead of classifying it, which involves selecting part of the field and ignoring the rest, it is theoretically conceivable that we might succeed in knowing directly the whole of the process of duration which constitutes the individual mental life of each one of us. And it is not even certain that our knowledge must necessarily be confined within the limits of what we have called our individual mental life. Particular facts, as we have seen, are not really distinct parts of a single individual mental life : the notion of separateness applies only to abstractions and it is only because we are much more pre-occupied with abstractions than with actual facts that we come to suppose that facts can ever really be separate from one another. When we shake off our common sense assumptions and examine the actual facts which we know directly we find that they form a process and not a logical series of distinct facts one after the other. Now on analogy it seems possible that what we call individual mental lives are, to the wider process which contains and constitutes the whole of reality, as particular facts are to the whole process which constitutes each individual mental life. The whole of reality may contain individual lives as these contain particular facts, not as separate distinct units in logical relations, but as a process in which the line of demarcation between " the parts " (if we must speak of " parts ") is not clear cut. If this analogy holds then it is impossible in advance to set any limits to the field of direct knowledge which it may be in our power to secure by reversing our usual mental attitude and devoting our energies simply to knowing, instead of to classifying and explaining.

But without going beyond the limits of our individual experience, and even without coming to know directly the whole field of past and present fact which that experience contains, it is still a considerable gain to our direct knowledge if we realize what false assumptions our preoccupation with classification leads us to make even about the very limited facts to which our direct knowledge is ordinarily confined. We then realize that, besides being considerably less than what we probably have it in our power to know, these few facts that we do know are themselves by no means what we commonly suppose them to be.

The two fundamental errors into which common sense leads us about the facts are the assumptions that they have the logical form, that is contain mutually exclusive parts in external relations, and that these parts can be repeated over and over again. These two false assumptions are summed up in the common sense view that the fact which we know directly actually consists of events, things, states, qualities. Bergson tells us that when once we have realized that this is not the case we have begun to be philosophers.

Having stripped the veil of common sense assumptions from what we know directly our task will then be to hold this direct knowledge before us so as to know as much as possible. The act by which we know directly is the very same act by which we perceive and remember; these are all simply acts of synthesis, efforts to turn matter into creative duration. What we have to do is, as it were, to make a big act of perception to embrace as wild a field as possible of past and present as a single fact directly known. This act of synthesis Bergson calls " intuition."

Intuition may be described as turning past and present into fact directly known by transforming it from mere matter into a creative process of duration: but, of course, actually, there is not, first matter, then an act of intuition which synthesises it, and finally a fact in duration, there is simply the duration, and the matter and the act of intuition are only abstractions by which we describe and explain it.

The effort of intuition is the reversal of the intellectual effort to abstract and explain which is our usual way of treating facts, and these two ways of attending are incompatible and cannot both be carried on together.

Intuition, (or, to give it a more familiar name, direct knowledge,) reveals fact: intellectual attention analyses and classifies this fact in order to explain it in general terms, that is to explain it by substituting abstractions for the actual fact. Obviously we cannot perform acts of analysis without some fact to serve as material: analysis uses the facts supplied by direct knowledge as its material. Bergson maintains that in so doing it limits and distorts these facts and he says that if we are looking for speculative knowledge we must go back to direct knowledge, or, as he calls it, intuition.

But bare acquaintance is in-communicable, moreover it requires a great effort to maintain it. In order to communicate it and retain the power of getting the facts back again after we have relaxed our grip on them we are obliged, once we have obtained the fullest direct knowledge of which we are capable, to apply the intellectual method to the fact thus revealed and attempt to describe it in general terms.

Now the directly known forms a creative duration whose special characteristics are that it is non-logical, (i.e., is not made up of distinct mutually exclusive terms united by external relations) and does not contain parts which can be repeated over and over, while on the other hand the terms which we have to substitute for it if we want to describe it only stand for repetitions and have the logical form. It looks, therefore, as if our descriptions could not, as they stand, be very successful in conveying to others the fact known to us directly, or in recalling it to ourselves.

In order that the description substituted by our intellectual activity for the facts which we want to describe may convey these facts it is necessary to perform an act of synthesis on the description analogous to the act of perception which originally created the fact itself out of mere matter. The words used in a description should be to the hearer what mere matter is to the perceiver : in order that matter may be perceived an act of synthesis must be performed by which the matter is turned into fact in duration : similarly in order to gather what a description of a fact means the hearer must take the general terms which are employed not as being distinct and mutually exclusive but as modifying one another and interpenetrating in the way in which the " parts " of a process of creative duration interpenetrate. In the same way by understanding the terms employed synthetically and not intellectually we can use a description to recall any fact which we have once known directly. Thus our knowledge advances by alternate acts of direct acquaintance and analysis.

Philosophy must start from a fresh effort

of acquaintance creating, if possible, a fact wider and fuller than the facts which we are content to know for the purposes of everyday life. But analysis is essential if the fact thus directly known is to be conveyed to others and recalled. By analysis the philosopher fixes this wider field in order that he may communicate and recall it. Starting later from the description of some fact obtained by a previous effort of acquaintance, or from several facts obtained at different times, and also from the facts described by others, and using all these descriptions as material, it may be possible, by a fresh effort, to perform acts of acquaintance, (or synthesis) embracing ever wider and wider fields of knowledge. This, according to Bergson, is the way in which philosophical knowledge should be built up, facts, obtained by acts of acquaintance, being translated into descriptions only that these descriptions may again be further synthesised so directing our attention to more and more comprehensive facts.

Inevitably, of course, these facts themselves, being less than all the stream of creative duration to which they belong, will be abstractions, if taken apart from that whole stream, and so distorted. This flaw in what we know even by direct acquaintance can never be wholly remedied short of our succeeding in becoming acquainted with the whole of duration. It is something, however, to be aware of the flaw, even if we cannot wholly remedy it, and the wider the acquaintance the less is the imperfection in the fact known.

The first step, in any case, towards obtaining the wider acquaintance at which philosophy aims consists in making the effort necessary to rid ourselves of the practical preoccupation which gives us our bias towards explaining everything long before we have allowed ourselves time to pay proper attention to it, in order that we may at least get back to such actual facts as we do already know directly. When this has been accomplished (and our intellectual habits are so deeply ingrained that the task is by no means easy) we can then go on to other philosophers' descriptions of the facts with which their own efforts to widen their direct knowledge have acquainted them and, by synthesising the general terms which they have been obliged to employ, we also may come to know these more comprehensive facts. Unless it is understood synthetically, however, a philosopher's description of the facts with which he has acquainted himself will be altogether unsatisfactory and misleading. It is in this way that Bergson's own analysis of the fact which we all know directly into matter and the act of memory by which matter is turned into a creative process should be understood.

The matter and the act of memory are both abstractions from the actual fact : he does not mean that over and above the fact there is either any matter or any force or activity called memory nor are these things supposed to be in the actual fact : they are simply abstract terms in which the fact is described.

Bergson tries elsewhere to put the same point by saying that there are two tendencies in reality, one towards space (that is logical form) and the other towards duration, and that the actual fact which we know directly "tends" now towards "space" and now towards duration. The two faculties intellect and intuition are likewise fictions which are not really supposed to exist, distinct from the fact to which they are applied, but are simply abstract notions invented for the sake of description.

Whatever the description by which a philosopher attempts to convey what he has discovered we shall only understand it if we remember that the terms in which the fact is described are not actually parts of the fact itself and can only convey the meaning intended if they are grasped by synthesis and not intellectually understood.

PRINTED IN GREAT BRITAIN BY THE DEVONSHIRE PRESS, TORQUAY